LA GLYCINE

Art Nouveau &
Art Deco
Fashion Postcards

Edith Weber

Covers and book designed by: Bruce Waters
Type set in Parisian-heading font/Arrus BT-text font

ISBN: 978-0-7643-3270-8
Printed in China

Schiffer Books are available at special discounts for bulk purchases for sales promotions or premiums. Special editions, including personalized covers, corporate imprints, and excerpts can be created in large quantities for special needs. For more information contact the publisher:

Published by Schiffer Publishing Ltd.
4880 Lower Valley Road
Atglen, PA 19310
Phone: (610) 593-1777; Fax: (610) 593-2002
E-mail: Info@schifferbooks.com

For the largest selection of fine reference books on this and related subjects, please visit our web site at
www.schifferbooks.com
We are always looking for people to write books on new and related subjects. If you have an idea for a book please contact us at the above address.

This book may be purchased from the publisher.
Include $5.00 for shipping.
Please try your bookstore first.
You may write for a free catalog.

In Europe, Schiffer books are distributed by
Bushwood Books
6 Marksbury Ave.
Kew Gardens
Surrey TW9 4JF England
Phone: 44 (0) 20 8392 8585; Fax: 44 (0) 20 8392 9876
E-mail: info@bushwoodbooks.co.uk
Website: www.bushwoodbooks.co.uk

Contents

Acknowledgements

As always, my son Barry, my daughter-in-law Sonja, and my grandson Adam, have been supportive and helpful in every way. Special thanks to Adam for his technical computer assistance.

Thanks to my brother, Cy Chermak, whose love always comforts me.

My thanks to Rod Kennedy for his help in getting this book off the ground, as well as for his guidance to its final hours.

Many thanks to Heidi Scheuber, and Estelle Jones for the friendship they graciously provided whenever I needed it.

Thanks to Christian Moulin, my great hair stylist, for translating the idioms on my French postcards to English.

As for my postcard "buddies" Phillip Van Aver, John Marioriu, Carlton Bloodgood, Ray and Edith Chase, Joan Kay, Agnes Cavallari, Susan Lane, and all the members of the Metropolitan Postcard Club, thank you for the many delightful postcard hours we have shared.

Preface

Perhaps some readers recognize the name, Edith Weber, as one of the foremost Antique jewelry dealers in the country. Perhaps they have even visited the "Edith Weber Fine Jewelry" shop in New York City. In any case, this book's author and that jewelry dealer are one and the same person! A far cry from picture postcards, you might say! But is it? Let's see.

In 1972, I joined two American friends who lived and worked in London by sharing their stand in one of the West End's permanent indoor antiques markets. One friend sold Oriental art while the other dealt in postcards; I stocked a small showcase with jewelry. I was, however, mostly a visiting partner.

I must admit I had very little respect for my friend's postcards. While postcards were one of the most popular London collectible, I had no patience with the time-consuming buyers who spent hours poring over countless boxes of cards, only to select a 50-pence ($1.00) view card! And I didn't try to hide my feelings. However, one evening my friend invited me to join him at a postcard auction, and I went.

At the viewing before the sale, I noticed a "lot" of 10 postcards. I recognized and was immediately attracted to their Art Nouveau designs. The cards each had a lovely lady wearing a different outfit representing an individual month of the year. They were all signed by the artist Alphonse Mucha.

When the lot came up for sale, I raised my hand and kept it up until the hammer came down; the cards were mine. Then and there, I made up my mind to look for and find the two missing cards and. A postcard collector was born!

I spent the next thirty years on buying trips throughout Europe. I divided my time between searching for wonderful Antique jewelry, and looking for marvelous Antique postcards. It has been a joyful ride!

The two "missing" postcards from the twelve "Months of the Year," July and August, are shown here.

The Missing Months

I can't recall exactly how long it took me to locate the two missing cards from the Mucha "Months of the Year" set, but I remember very clearly the unbelievable joy and exhilaration when the set was finally completed. My main goal became, and remains to this day, to collect complete sets of rare and marvelous postcards.

The Art Nouveau Movement: 1898-1916

Translating from the French, "Art Nouveau" literally means "New Art". It was a revolt against the rigid and strict rules, as well as the confining fashions, of the Victorian era. Artists working in every medium, at various times, in almost every country, embraced Art Nouveau designs.

This revolution was most immediately evident in Women's Fashion. Stifling corsets were discarded, and replaced by loose flowing robes.The prim Victorian tight knot of hair at the top of the head, was unpinned and hair was allowed to fall free.

Art Nouveau was typified by lovely ladies wearing loose dresses, with their hair accented by flowers in artistically undulating floral designs. We will compare two postcards that illustrate this metamorphosis.

The Victorian lady, on the right, is about to get dressed. She gives us a glimpse of her constricting whale-bone corset. As soon as she is dressed, she will most probably put her hair up in a tight knot. The Art Nouveau lady, on the left, is wearing a billowy dress and her hair, trimmed with flowers, hangs down to her waist.

We will now go on to look at the great Art Nouveau postcard artists, and their ROMANCE with Fashion.

A Victorian lady

An Art Nouveau lady

Alphonse Mucha

The Beginning Period

It is only fitting that the Art Nouveau section of this book begins with Mucha, who is truly the "father of the Art Nouveau movement." Alphonse Mucha was born in Moravia, Czechoslovakia, in 1850. He knew by the time he was a teenager that he wanted to be a painter. Like every aspiring artist of his day, Mucha ended up in Paris in 1887. A Czech patron from Moravia funded his first two years there, before the money was abruptly discontinued. Mucha was left adrift in Paris. He had no money and no prospects. He was the proverbial starving artist.

For five years he struggled without support and living on lentils. He scrounged for odd painting jobs to pay for the medicines to keep himself alive.

In 1895, over the Christmas holiday when nobody else was available, he was given an assignment to create a poster for a new play that starred actress Sarah Bernhardt.

He designed a full-length poster of her in a style he had long been developing. This "new" art style featured her in a soft, flowing, pastel gown and with long, loose, undulating hair. With it, the "Art Nouveau" (new art) movement exploded in the art world!

Designs For A Menu

The famous posters of Sarah Bernhardt, who was the most popular actress in the world in 1895 and was known as "The Divine Sarah," were eventually turned into postcards. An early set of four designs is known as "Designs For A Menu".

A postcard of Sarah Bernhardt in the play *La Samaritaine*

The Middle Period

The first Mucha poster of Sarah Bernhardt was an immediate sensation! It sold over 8,000 copies when it appeared, and overnight the Mucha name became a household word in France. Art Nouveau was commonly referred to as "Le Style Mucha".

Commissions poured in and his fame spread around the world. His trips to America resulted in magazine covers, illustrations, and portraits. Many of his posters were printed as postcards and they, too, sold by the thousands.

Two of Mucha's famous designs that were printed as postcards are "Design for a Fan" and "Design for a Soirée".

Design for a fan

Design for a soirée

The Final Period

Alphonse Mucha was always a patriot of his homeland, Czechoslovakia. In 1909 he began a series of paintings illustrating the major events in the nation's history. The series took eighteen years to complete and was presented to the city of Prague in 1928.

His fellow country-men were not kind to Mucha. His bequest to his country was received with unkindly, cold shoulders. Although his work was beautiful and even popular, it was by then no longer "new," a failing in the eyes of the critics.

When the German army invaded Czechoslovakia, he was still influential enough to be one of the first people arrested. He returned home after a Gestapo questioning session and died shortly thereafter, on July 14, 1939.

Two more of his famous designs became postcards. They are his "Design For The Magazine *Cocorico*" and his "Design For A Calendar."

Design for the magazine Cocorico

Design for a calendar

Jack Abeillé

Jack Abeillé was born in France in 1873. By 1898, he was a well-established cartoonist and illustrator and turned his attention to designing postcards.

The popular cards of this period were small, multiple images of towns or cities, known as "Gruss aus" cards. Abeillé, however, was more interested in art, and particularly fashion.

Fashion Through the Ages

He designed a series of postcards that illustrate his concept of fashion through the ages. Not only did he sign these cards, he also dated them [18]98. He was a true pioneer. The two cards shown here illustrate his concept of fashion for the years 1540 and 1760. Both show these dates on their fronts.

The remaining cards are his interpretations of fashions in the 13th century, the 17th century, and the English Restoration.

Evangeline (Eva) Danielle

Biographical details of Eva Danielle's life are virtually unknown. It has been determined, however, that she was born in 1880 and died in 1902, at the very young age of 22.

Unfortunately, not a great deal is known about her work. It is known that she created postcards entitled "Modern Art" Post Card series #2525, and "Art" Post Card series #2524, both for Raphael Tuck & Sons, the prominent London publisher.

Because she died at such a young age, there are not many examples of her outstanding artistry available today. The fact that she rarely signed her cards makes it even more difficult to identify her work.

Two cards from her "Art" Series #2524 and four cards from her "Modern Art" Series #2525 appear on these pages.

A Happy Christmas to you from

A Happy
Christmas
to you
from

To my
dear little
sweet little
Valentin

Arpad Basch

Arpad Basch was born in Budapest, Hungary, in 1873. As a young man he studied painting in Budapest, Munich, and Paris, and in 1896 he returned to Hungary. He had become an accomplished artist and had no problem getting work there. Not only did he get assignments as a commercial artist, but he became a popular illustrator for many books, almanacs, and magazines.

"Female Warriors"

During this time he became interested in the newly developing market for designing postcards. He began with designs for popular *Gruss aus* view cards, but before long he turned his attention to the emerging Art Nouveau style. In 1900 he created one of his most famous sets of fashion postcards, a six-card series that is commonly known as "Female Warriors." He signed these cards "Basch, Arpad 1900," in an era when very few artists signed and dated their cards. Cards from this set are shown.

13

Arpad Basch

Ernest Louis Lessieux

E. Louis Lessieux was born in La Rochelle, France, in 1848. He was a multi-talented artist and he had no difficulty finding employment as a commercial artist, an oil painter, and a watercolorist. He was a professor of design at the high school at La Rochefort.

Precious Stones

Lessieux began to specialize in watercolors. From 1878 he put them on exhibit, where they received a good deal of recognition. We don't know when he first became interested in designing postcards, but one of his most famous postcard sets, Precious Stones, was designed in 1900 and printed in 1901.

This set is so softly colored that it appears to be painted with watercolors. If you look closely, you will see that the Art Nouveau gowns worn by the lovely ladies are enhanced by gorgeous Art Nouveau jewels, each containing its specific "Precious Stone." The Stones are named on the fronts of the cards. "Topaz" and "Pearl" are shown here.

L'EMERAUDE

LE DIAMANT

LA TURQUOISE

L'AGATE

Alexandre Theodore Steinlen

Alexander Theodore Steinlen was born in Lousanne, France, in 1859, and in 1923, at the age of 64, he died in Paris.

Steinlen was the grandson of the painter Christian Gottlieb. He was a multi-talented artist: a painter, designer of fabrics and porcelains, as well as a theatrical set designer and costumer. Between 1879 and 1881, he worked as a fabric designer while painting porcelains with designs taken from his grandfather's watercolors.

In 1881 he moved to Paris, where he designed theatrical sets and costumes. A lack of documentation regarding his postcards makes it difficult to establish whether his cards were original designs (as most experts believe) or reproductions from the illustrations he did for French magazines. It really doesn't matter, because the world he depicted in magazine articles also appeared in his best postcards.

Fashions of the Ordinary Lady

He was a painter of daily life, an artist of the streets. The groups of people sitting at pavement tables show us the simple clothing of ordinary French ladies. No "femme fatale" here, no dazzling gowns, no stunning accessories, no blazing jewelry. Steinlen was a dedicated interpreter of the world of the urban poor. He shows pedestrian fashions of unfashionable ladies plodding along in their heavy practical shoes. Four of his famous postcards are pictured.

A Parisian working girl

Henri Meunier

Henri Meunier was born in Belgium in 1873. He was the son of the engraver Jean Baptiste Meunier, and he completed his early art studies under the guidance of his father.

He first exhibited his engravings in 1890 and he continued to exhibit until 1897. At this time he was designing covers and illustrations for several magazines. Most of his commercial work, including his postcards, were done for the publisher Dietrich, in Brussels.

Meunier did not always sign his work. When and if his postcards were signed, it was only with his initials, M over H.

Two cards shown are named and signed examples of the Art Nouveau lady with the flowing hair that he helped popularize.

"Beauty"

"Inspiration"

Attributed Coiffeurs

Meunier was equally fascinated by unique ways of accessorizing Art Nouveau flowing hair. These three cards that illustrate unusual hairstyling have been attributed to Meunier.

Raphael Kirchner

Raphael Kirchner was born in Vienna, Austria, in 1876. He began his artistic career as a portrait painter of women. Around 1900 he settled in Paris, where his first postcards were published; they were immediately successful. Biographers describe Kirchner's women as the first "pin-up girls," but some critics point out that most of his ladies look alike. In fact, he used his lovely wife, Nina, as his model. We can only assume that Nina wore her hair with flowers at her ears, as that is the most popular fashion hairstyle of Kirchner's ladies.

Fashion Series
Six cards from Kirchner's fashion series are shown.

Raphael Kirchner is said to have created about a thousand different designs for postcards for Austrian, German, French, English, and even some American publishers. One of his popular series had four successful reprints, reaching 40,000 copies. He was so prolific that biographers suggest that his wife, Nina, may have helped him keep up with the huge demand by painting some of the images herself.

Cigarettes of the World

In 1900 Kirchner published a unique set of six cards entitled "Les Cigarettes Du Monde," which translates to English as "Cigarettes of the World." Each card features a lady wearing a unique Fashion outfit that represents and characterizes a different cigarette, from a different country. The cards are numbered and the cigarette brands are named on the front of each card.

Samuel L. Schmucker

Samuel L. Schmucker is an American postcard artist whose work has the same exquisite beauty and creativity as the great European artists. He was born in 1879, in Pennsylvania, and studied art from 1896-1900, in the United States. His passion was art, even though his right arm had been crippled by polio in childhood. He adopted a claw-like grip and held the brush between his right index and second fingers, with movement coming from his arm. Schmucker died in 1921, at the age of 42. Unfortunately, he did not receive the recognition to which he was entitled.

Butterfly Ladies

One of Schmucker's most lovely series, Butterfly Ladies, was submitted as original paintings to the Detroit Publishing Company in 1907. The images were subsequently published as postcards, but the original artwork was lost, until recently. Schmucker used the butterfly to symbolize the union of a lovely Art Nouveau lady with nature. In his inimitable awareness of fashion, he dressed his creatures elegantly. Each card in this series has a faint title on the front.

Entitled, "Inconstancy"

Entitled, "Elusoriness"

Entitled, "L'Envoi".

Entitled, "Sensibility"

Entitled, "Fragility"

Holidays

In the United States, during the height of "postcard mania," postcards that celebrate holidays were among the most popular. Schmucker produced many postcards of this type, the majority copyrighted and published by John Winsch.

While other American artists portrayed the Hallowe'en witch as an ugly, old crone with scraggly white hair, sometimes dressed in a ragged cape and hat, Schmucker's witches are young, pretty, and dressed in the height of fashion.

Christmas cards show ladies dressed as
"Holly," Poinsettia," and "Mistletoe."

Serge de Solomko

Serge de Solomko was of Russian origin, but few details of his life are known. He worked primarily in Paris as a painter and illustrator, and for a time he worked for the magazine *Jugend,* and illustrated several books for French publishers.

Sometime before the Russian revolution, his cards dealt with Russian subjects and Russian fashion, although they were published primarily in France,.

The backs of his postcards contain a small paragraph with his name and the title of the card in Russian and English. In some cases, the information is in Russian, German, French, and English.

Fashions of Average Russians

In these postcards by Serge de Solomko, notice the abundance of lush fabrics, intricate designs, and patterns.

Russian Princesses

He also examined fashions of the princesses of the opulent Russian court.

Art Nouveau Advertising

A budding advertising market emerged during the 1900s, brought on by the phenomenal popularity of postcard collecting. The best artists in Europe were hired to create images for advertisements on postcards.

La Belle Jardiniere

The set of six cards featured here advertises "La Belle Jardiniere," a prominent lady's accessory shop in Paris. The shop's name and address is printed across the bottom of the front and on the top of the back of each card.

While this lovely series is unsigned, it is sometimes erroneously attributed to Mucha. The mistake exists because Mucha created a similar series for the same shop, but he signed his cards.

This unsigned series, showing lovely ladies dressed in outfits that represent different flowers, is too exciting to ignore. The flowers shown include Chrysanthemum, Iris, Rose, and Christmas Rose.

Entitled,"Glycine" (wisteria)

Entitled, "Pavot" (poppy)

CHRYSANTHÈME

Souvenir de la Belle Jardinière
2, Rue du Pont-Neuf, PARIS.

LA ROSE

Souvenir de la Belle Jardinière
2, Rue du Pont-Neuf, PARIS.

LA ROSE de NOËL

Souvenir de la Belle Jardinière
2, Rue du Pont-Neuf, PARIS.

The Art Deco Movement: 1917-1930

The term "Art Deco" is an abbreviation of the French words, "Art Decoratif". This movement, like the Art Nouveau movement, was a revolt against the style of the times. While Art Nouveau revolted against the rigidity of Victorianism, Art Deco rebelled against the bland colors and soft curving lines of Art Nouveau.

Artists became interested in working in a more dynamic and vibrant style. The "Roaring Twenties" was the perfect climate for the Art Deco movement. Women cut their hair short, and along with their "bobbed" hair they wore striking outfits in geometric designs of bright, bold colors.

Alongside of the bright colors of Art Deco, the Art Nouveau lady seems to have become drab and unexciting. Our Deco lady, however, is a chic, cigarette-smoking, be-jeweled and sophisticated "Flapper!"

On the next page, two unsigned Art Nouveau and two unsigned Art Deco cards are contrasted. The remainder of the book will be devoted to Art Deco FASHION postcards and the innovative artists who created them!!

Art Nouveau vs. Art Deco Fashion

The Art Nouveau Lady

The Art Deco Lady

Umberto Brunelleschi

Umberto Brunelleschi was born in Montemurlo, Italy, in 1879. He studied painting and sculpture at the Academia di Belle Arte in Florence. In 1901, he moved to Paris. In 1912, he made his debut as a set designer for the ballet "Legende da Clair da Lune."

This ballet influence is seen in one of his most famous series of six postcards entitled "Femme" (Lady). His lovely Art Deco ladies seem to move with the grace of ballerinas. The charming outfits he created for these ladies, though risqué, seem to carry out the balletic theme. These postcards were published in France, and numbered series 31 on the backs, where each card is given a title.

Entitled,"Femme au Mirroir" (lady and mirror)

Entitled, "Femme á la Petrouche" (lady and birdcage)

Brunelleschi's studio in Paris became the meeting place for the great personalities of the world of Art and culture. Such famous artists as Modigliani, Picasso, Belldini, and D'Annunzio were frequent guests at his Studio. In 1914, at the outbreak of World War I, he returned to Italy and joined the army.

In 1918, when the war ended, he returned to Paris, where he worked as a set designer for the Follies Bergère, The Casino, and for the Thêatre de Paris. Although many of his postcards were published in Italy, he lived in Paris until his death in 1949.

The four remaining cards from this enchanting series are titled: "Femme au Papillon" (Lady and Butterfly), "Femme a l'Oiseau" (Lady and Bird, "Femme a l'Eventail"(Lady and Fan), and "Femme a la Violette" (Lady and Violet).

Suffragettes

Brunelleschi was living in Paris in the early 20th century as women were fighting for the right to vote. A unique set of cards he designed at this time portrays women suffragettes. The six-card set shows ladies, wearing charming clothes he designed for them, as they perform jobs that were formerly considered tasks for men only. Brunelleschi did not title these cards, however, each lady seems to be doing a man's job, including the Mail Lady, the Lady Street Cleaner, the Lady Train Conductor, and the Lady Carriage Driver.

The Lady Baggage Carrier

The Lady Barber

M. (Marcello?) Montedoro

By the beginning of the Art Deco movement, the hobby of collecting postcards had become a public addiction. Most cards were printed in Germany, the world leader in the process of chromolithography. However, at the height of the world-wide mania, World War I caused the hobby to crash. Since Germany was the enemy, the supply of Art postcards came to an abrupt end in the Allied countries.

Fortunately, a small group of artists in Italy kept the high standard of design flourishing during the "Jazz Age". This happened at a time when most other cards had become dull, unimaginative, and poorly or cheaply produced. One of the most creative artists of this group was M. Montedoro.

Unfortunately, there is very little biographical information about Montedoro. We are not even sure of his first name. But some facts derive from the publisher of an exciting series of fashion postcards. We know it was published in Milan, the publisher dates each card 1917, and numbers on the backs of the cards are B-1 through B-6.

Mela Koehler

Melanie (Mela) Koehler was born in Vienna, Austria, in 1885. She studied and worked there as part of the prestigious art school , the Wiener Workstatte (Vienna Workshop), which boasted the foremost teachers and artisans in the arts.

Koehler was a designer of fabrics and ceramics. In addition, she designed 150 fashion postcards. Several Austrian publishers featured her postcards, and her art work was exhibited both in magazines and on tour. She was very successful, and died in 1960.

Two postcards illustrating her wonderful use of fabric design as background for her unique Fashions are shown here. It is interesting to note that she throws in the cute little doggies as an extra attraction.

Fashion Fabrics

Of all the artists who designed postcards for the Wiener Workstatte, Mela Koehler's work was the most popular. Her unique approach to Art Deco fashion, which she combined with innovative fabric designs, endeared her work to women of the era.

Hats

One of Koehler's most famous fashion sets is a series of six cards that show exciting and chic hats to be worn with bobbed (short) hair styles.

Hats were not an afterthought to Art Deco designers, but an integral part of every outfit. They were designed for every occasion and for various needs.

This set was published by B.K.W.I. It was printed in Austria, series #481. It is interesting to note the fabrics she designed to be used in conjunction with her hat designs. The remaining four cards from the "Hat" series are illustrated on the next two pages.

Léo Fontan

Léo Fontan was born in the French Ardennes region, in 1884. As a boy he decided that he would be a painter. He studied at the School of Fine Arts and then went to Paris where he became a part of the city's artistic and bohemian community. He was a member of the League of French Artists from 1911 to 1946, joined the Libraire de l'estampe where he replaced Raphael Kirchner, and began to draw "small women" (postcards featuring women}.

Léo Fontan had one of the world's most brilliant leg fetishes. We have him to thank for first-hand knowledge of hosiery and shoes of the day, as well as the gorgeous legs of Art Deco women!

Despite failing eyesight, Fontan continued to paint until the last day of his life in 1965.

One typical set of seven cards, Series #17, is entitled "Les Bas Transparant" (Sheer Stockings). In its day, this set was considered risqué.

Story of a pair of Legs

Another of Fontan's popular sets, Series #87, is entitled, "Histoire d'une paire de jambs," (Story of a pair of Legs).

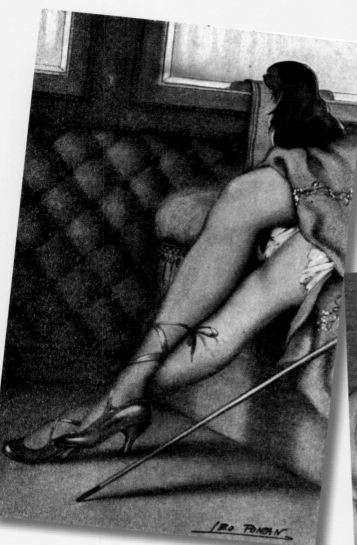

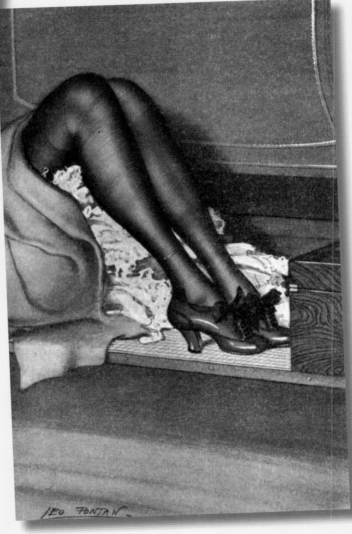

Enrico Sacchetti

Enrico Sacchetti was born in Rome, Italy, in 1877. He received his diploma at the Instituto Technico and studied art in Florence, but he was mainly self-taught. He worked as an illustrator and caricaturist for newspapers and journals of Milan. From 1908 to 1911 he lived in Buenos Aires, where he worked for the newspaper *El Diaro*. Later, he went to France for three years, and was active mainly as a fashion designer. At the outbreak of World War I he returned to Italy.

During the war years he designed postcards featuring his original fashions. He spent the rest of his life in Florence, where he died in 1967 at the age of 90.

Fashion Designs

A remarkable set of postcards illustrating his unique fashion designs was published by Zeniti. The series is numbered 25 and dated 1917 by the publisher.

Luigi Bompard

Luigi Bompard was born in Bologna, Italy, in 1879. He established himself there with illustrations he made in 1900, then worked successively for the famous magazines *L'illustration Italiana* and *Illustration Francaise*. He also made illustrations for books, including *The Conquest of the South Pole*, by explorer E. H. Shackleton.

Art Deco Fashion

By 1915 he was well established as a fashion designer and became interested in designing postcards with the accent on fashion. We have no evidence that the outfits on his fashion postcards were his designs, but that may be the case.

A series of fashion postcards, numbered 991, was published in Milan and dated 1918 on the backs by the publisher.

Fall Fashion

Bompard lived for a long time in Paris, where he was influenced by many of his fashion-designing friends. This influence is particularly evident in Bompard's series of engravings "Fashionable Life," which he exhibited in Rome in 1915 and in London in 1916. As a painter, Bompard exhibited his work at the Venice Biennales in 1905, 1912 and 1920.

Bompard was relatively successful during this time and moved to Rome, where he concentrated on creating postcards, particularly cards with fashion subject. He spent the rest of his life in Rome, until his death in 1953.

The Leaves of October

A six-card set of his fashion postcards was published in Milan. It features clothing outfits complimented by small fur pelts and fur scarves, still known today as stoles.

There is no publisher indicated on the cards, nor is the date of publication known; only a series number, 515, is printed. Most likely, the set was printed around 1918. It has no title, but I have always thought of it as *The Leaves of October.*

Sofia Chiostri

Sofia Chiostri was born in Italy, in 1898. She taught design in the Educandato of the Announced, in Florence. Her father, Carlo, was a self-taught illustrator who became famous because of his illustrations for the first publication of the book *Pinocchio*. Carlo Chiostri signed his work "C.C." He sometimes used a pseudonym, so as not to infringe on Sophia's budding fame.

Between teaching and a simple, calm life, Sofia created wonderful postcards in a strong Art Deco style. She signed her cards "Chiostri," perhaps because her father was so famous, but also perhaps because designing postcards was not considered an appropriate career for a woman at that time.

Although most postcard series are created in a set of six cards (or occasionally seven cards) around a central theme, Sophia preferred to make only four cards to a series. Most of her work was published by Ballerini & Fratini of Firenze (Florence), Italy.

Her series #245, in which Cherubs powder and perfume a fashionable Art Deco lady, are characteristic of her work.

Fashions for a Bathing Beauty

Three cards are from series #181, in which Chiostri illustrates her dramatic fashions for a bathing beauty.

After the war, both Carlo Chiostri and Sofia Chiostri found it difficult to continue working as artists. Carlo died in 1939, and in 1945 Sophia died in Florence, from the suffering and hardships of the war.

All of her postcards were produced in Italy, and are identified by her striking colors and personal view of Art Deco fashions.

Months of the Year

One of her most famous series is the set *Months of the Year*, series #258. Each card features the birthstone, horoscope sign, and an Art Deco lady in an outfit suitable for the month.

February

January

Sofia Chiostri

67

Luciano A. Mauzan

Luciano A. Mauzan was born in the high Alpes region near the German-Italian border in 1883. He received a diploma with a gold medal in 1905 and traveled through Italy before settling in Milan and working as a commercial artist.

He rapidly became one of the country's most popular designers of cinema posters. During the war years, he began designing postcards. From 1917 to 1946, he designed more than a thousand original postcards, many with fashions and fashionable women as the motifs. During his long and distinguished career he also designed over two thousand posters. He divided his life between Milan, Paris, and Buenos Aires. He returned to France for his last years and died there in 1952.

Fashion Series

The chic, six-card fashion series, #278, was published in Milan and dated 1917.

Tito Corbella

Tito Corbella was born in Pontgremoli, Italy, in 1885. He earned a degree in chemistry at the University of Padua, but became interested in and studied art in Venice, where he began his painting career. He also worked as an illustrator and commercial artist.

Corbella became famous for designing postcards that feature women of fashion. His many series display the outstanding styles of women's clothing and accessories worn during the Art Deco period. His cards were published in Italy. The publishers and dates of publication are not known. Corbella began designing fashion postcards in 1914 and continued to produce them until the 1920s. During his lifetime, he created over 300 postcard designs. He may have used his wife as his inspiration and model for many of his portraits of women. In his later years he continued to produce postcards, but he also designed posters for the famous poster publisher Ricordi.

Feathers

Postcard series #130, which is not dated, features lovely ladies wearing feather accessories in short, waved, hair syles, known as "marcelled" hair.

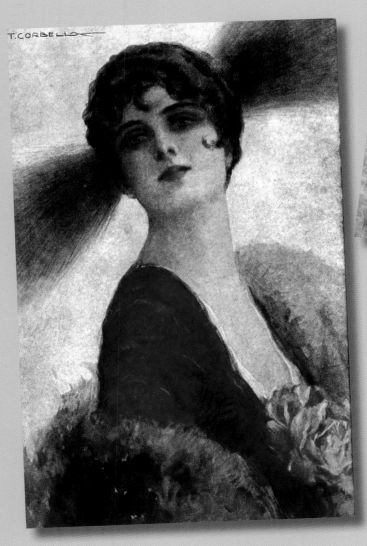

Headgear

A hat fashion that became popular during the Art Deco period was the turban. It went around the head and came down over the ears. A six-card series, # 467, features Corbella's designs for winter turbans. The series was published by Dell'Anna & Gasparini, of Milan.

Two cards from this set show ladies in winter wraps, topped off with turbans.

Be-jeweled Turbans

Four cards, from series # 306 by Corbella, show
ladies wearing be-jeweled turbans.

Designs For A Performer

Corbella also produced other fashion postcards that are not illustrations of real ladies wearing chic clothes and accessories, but seem to be Corbella's designs for a stage performer. Could they have been created for Sally Rand? She was the most famous name in live burlesque theatre during the 1930s. Her legendary Fan Dance raised the level of the "strip tease" to an art form. In 1934, she danced at the Chicago World's Fair, where she created a sensation.

There is no documentation that Corbella had Sally Rand in mind when he created the exciting Art Deco postcards that were published by Dagami as series #2109. They are signed, as he signed all of his cards, "T. Corbella."

I prefer to believe they are Corbella's interpretation of how the First Lady of Burlesque should be dressed, as she stands in front of the curtain holding her famous fan.

Giovanni Nanni

Giovanni Nanni was born in Italy, in 1888. He was a painter and illustrator active in the mid-1900 period. He died in Italy in 1969.

Nanni is well known for postcards showing beautiful women adorned with wonderful hats and wrapped in splendid fur scarves of Art Deco style. Nanni stressed the vital role hats played as fashions in their own right. Many of his hat designs were combined with scarves; he usually ignored the models from the neck down.

Hats and Scarves

A six-card set of postcards by Nanni, series #304 published in Milan and dated 1918, shows hats combined with fur scarves. Be sure to notice that the women each wear "beauty marks." The height of cosmetic fashion at the time was to apply a dark accent mark with a cosmetic pencil, close to one eye.

Nanni produced a large amount of fashion oriented postcards during his life, but he is also famous for his special designs for advertising postcards, which he created for big Italian manufacturing companies.

Good Luck Symbols

While an Art Deco postcard series that features hats or scarves is not unusual, a series that features hats and scarves with good luck symbols is definitely unique. One thing that set Nanni's work apart from that of his colleagues was his use of fashion subjects that other artists working in Italy ignored.

A series that includes hats and scarves with good luck symbols, #284, was published in Milan and dated by the publisher 1917.

A pig, seen as a good luck charm in Italy,
is featured on this scarf.

A spider, considered good luck in Italy,
is featured on this scarf.

Xavier Sager

Paris in the early part of the twentieth century was considered the cultural and artistic center of the western world. An artist famous for his view of fashion, in the most fashionable city, was Xavier Sager, who also had a subtle sense of humor. Few biographical facts relating to his early life survive, except that he was born in Austria around 1870. He did most of his work in Paris and is known above all else for his postcard designs. It is calculated that he designed about 3,000 different cards, with a total issue of 3,000,000 examples. Sager continued to produce large amounts of postcards until his death in 1930.

Two fashion postcards, #8020 and #8021, are shown.

Bewitching.

Fashion for the Tango

Sager's designs on cards published by B.G., Paris, Series #474, illustrate his design for appropriate dress for performing a tango, the most popular dance of the day. One card from this series (the one without small dancers) is an example of Sager's satirical sense of humor. Notice how the man's hand has found its way downward from the lady's back!

Le Tango (gardez vos distances)

Le Double Boston

Fashionable Paris Ladies

As well as portraying current fashions, Xavier Sager delighted in exploring the lives and foibles of people in the Paris "high society." While he invented caricatures of fashion, he took even greater liberty creating scenes that depicted relationships between ladies and their gentlemen admirers. Sager's depictions are subtle and deliciously humorous. Although he poked fun, his characters never lost touch with reality.

Five of the cards in this genre, published by B.G., Paris, Series #545, are presented here. One is "La Femme Fatale," in which you will notice the rejected suitors on their knees, blowing their brains out! The second card is "Mutual Attractions," in which a man offering sacks of money and a tiny lady at the bottom who reads from a long list of her demands.

La Femme Fatale

Mutual Attractions

L'Amoureuse (the beloved)

La Seductrice (the seductress)

La Glace (ice)

Fashion and Dogs

Many Art Deco artists liked to use dogs in their postcards. They favored big, beautiful dogs like the Russian Wolfhound, which were so popular in this era. Sager used both cute little doggies and large, magnificent, white dogs. He preferred to keep the big dogs as a faint background to his colorful fashion designs and used the small dogs to create a subtly humorous effect. He sometimes selected a breed that looked something like the lady on the card, or he added an accessory to make it seem as though the dog was dressed like the lady.

The set with small dogs is published by B.G. Paris, series #588. All of the cards from this series are entitled "Fleur d'Hiver" (Flower of Winter). The series with large dogs is series #580.

Fleur d'hiver

Fleur d'hiver

Not too fast.

Ta-Ta!

The War Years

There are no records to identify the particular dates for the tremendous number of postcards designed by Xavier Sager. He began around 1900 to 1910, but did not produce typically Art Nouveau cards at this time. During the general period of World War I (1914 to 1918), the following two postcards were published by A. Noyer as Paris series #60, entitled "Leurs Poupées Nouvelles" (Their New Dolls).

Leurs Poupées Nouvelle (their new dolls)

Today's Idols

Sager's delightful sense of humor is revealed as the cards depict semi-clad ladies dropping ordinary men in favor of the soldiers they clutch in their arms. His humor is so subtle you have to look closely to see his partially hidden and sometimes naughty small jokes. This set is series #63, entitled "Les Idoles du Jour" (Today's Idols).

Stratégie

Strategy

Xavier Sager's Imitators

Xavier Sager had many imitators in Paris, including George Mouton, but their work lacks Sager's subtlety and beauty of design.

Because Sager was so often imitated, but never equaled, it is challenging and satisfying to compare his work with the artists who copied him. Notice that the imitators' designs for hairstyles and hats have little or no basis in reality. Therefore, there is no humor in them.

Two cards by Sager's imitators, illustrating hairstyles of 1909-1910, are shown.

Hair style by Robé.

Hair style by C. Ravok

Four postcards that are designed by George Mouton (one of Sager's most prolific imitators) illustrate hat fashions. He signed his cards "G. Mouton" and dated them "1909."

Alice Wanke

Alice Wanke was born in Vienna, Austria, in 1873. She studied art with Franz von Matsch in Vienna, and turned her attention to postcard design early in the 1900s. She was influenced by Xavier Sager's caricatures and began to create postcards that exaggerate, and even ridicule, the popular fashions in Vienna. As is the case with the French imitators, Wanke's work lacks subtlety. Nor was she as prolific or popular as Sager, but her willingness to create postcards that poke fun of the fashions of her day, is a testament to Sager's influence.

Biographers seem to have to have lost track of Wanke after 1909, but we know that she died in Vienna in 1936.

Fashion Caricatures

Alice Wanke's cards from a six-card set, numbered #452 and published by M.Monk in Vienna, are shown. A little square on the front bottom left of each card in the series bears her name and the date 1909.

Alice Wanke

Unsigned Postcards

Beginning collectors tend to shy away from unsigned cards, afraid they are of inferior quality; but that is not always the case. Outstanding artists, such as Samuel L. Schmucker and Henri Meunier, did not always sign their work.

Unsigned postcards force a buyer to judge for himself about a card's quality. Additionally, unsigned cards are usually more plentiful and often less costly than signed cards.

Unsigned cards are a good way to start getting interested in postcards. Generally, for a surprisingly small investment, the novice can accumulate a remarkable number of wonderful postcards. There is no substitute for the hours of pure joy that postcard hunting can bring.

The two unsigned cards shown on this page are compelling close-up studies of the hairstyles of an Art Nouveau lady and an Art Deco lady.

Art Nouveau lady with pearls in her hair

Art Deco lady, entitled "La Coiffeur"

Unsigned Art Deco Evening Gowns

The unsigned set of four postcards shows stunning evening gowns.

Appendix

Brief History of Postcards

To fully understand postcard collecting, we need to look at a brief pictorial history of how the hobby developed and grew.

Postcards were to the common man what T.V. and films are to us today. Postcards reflected life. They commented on everything. They came in an endless flow, running into countless of millions. These numbers were fed by the widespread and fashionable hobby of collecting them. Almost every household boasted at least one album in which the entire household hoarded its precious collection.

Pioneer Cards 1889-1898

Pioneer cards are the earliest postcards. They were mostly European "Gruss aus" cards. "Gruss aus" translates from the German to "Greetings from." They were truly greetings that contained small multiple scenes of a city or town. The entire back of the card was used for the address only. No message was allowed on this back side.

Pioneer cards, if they were mailed [postally used] frequently have writing all over the front, as there was no other place to write a message. Some collectors prefer unused cards with no writing, I know I do, but they are not easy to find. Such an unused "Gruss aus" card is seen here.

American Pioneer Cards 1889-1898

Most Pioneer cards were not popular in America. They pictured multiple views of virtually every European city. Americans, however, were not yet caught up in the postcard craze, and were certainly not interested in cards featuring European Cities. American pioneer cards did, however, exist, but they were rare.

It is interesting to note that the American pioneer card pictured here, translated "Gruss aus" to the American, "Greetings from" Boston. The back, reserved for address only, is unused, and therefore completely blank.

Private Mailing Cards 1898-1901

As of May 19, 1898 the government gave private printers permission to both sell, and print postcards inscribed with the words, "PRIVATE MAILING CARD", on the back. The back still could be used only for the address.

Not all cards, however, had such fancy backs as the card shown here. Private mailing cards were printed for such a short period of time that they are rarely seen today.

Undivided Back Cards 1901-1907

As of Dec.24, 1901 printers were allowed to use the words "POST CARD" on the back of their cards. Only the address, however, was written there. Postcard publishing during this time doubled almost every six months. European publishers opened offices in the USA and began importing millions of quality postcards.

Most postcards were printed in Germany, the world leader in the exquisite printing process known as "chromolithography". By 1907, European publishers accounted for over 75% of all postcards sold in this country. Cards were designed and printed in sets of four, six, (by far the most popular] and seven [mostly Italian) cards to a set or series. Each series was based around a common theme.

The card shown here (front and back) is an early undivided back card published by Raphael Tuck & sons, the prominent English publishing company.

Divided Back Cards 1907-1915

This era is known as "The Golden Age of Post-cards." As of March 1, 1907, the divided back postcard came into being. A line was drawn down the middle of the back of a card. The right hand side was for the address, and the left side for a message! It quickly became popular because it allotted a place for a message. At this time in history, the postcard collecting hobby became a national addiction.

Accumulating postcards became the greatest collectible hobby that the world has ever known. The official Post Office figures for the fiscal year ending June, 1908, lists 677,777,798 post cards mailed. This is a huge number, at a time when the total population of the U.S. was only 88,700,000!

Evaluating Postcards

This guide evaluates the current market values of the postcards pictured in this book. To fully understand, readers must realize that the "fair market value," as defined by the U. S. Internal Revenue Service, is the "price paid by a willing buyer to a willing seller."

This price, however, is not constant. Value is a fluctuating, non-fixed entity. It varies geographically from city to city, and from country to country. It changes according to many factors.

The venue in which a postcard is sold can cause price differences. Prices may vary according to whether a card is sold in a dealer's shop, at a postcard auction, in a show, or at a flea market.

Value will usually depend on the rarity of the postcard, as well as the fame of its artist. Sometimes, price will be determined by the popularity of the card's subject matter. The final factor, and the one that is the most easily recognizable, is its condition.

Postcard Condition

Cards with serious faults (rips, holes, missing corners, or major creases) are practically worthless. Postcards with minor flaws (such as slight ageing, or small writing on the front that does not mar the image) are usually rated to be in "Good "to "Very Good "condition. Cards with no visible flaws are considered to be in "Excellent" to "Near Mint" condition.

The condition of all the postcards in this book, range from "Good" to "Near Mint" condition. They have been purchased in many venues from around the world. They have been evaluated by taking ALL of the many variables into consideration. Then, relying on thirty years experience, the dollar range into which the postcard falls in *today's* market, has been determined.

The guide lists postcards by artists (or in the case of unsigned cards, by category). Listings are alphabetical, with the last name of the artist appearing first. A price range will be listed first for an individual postcard, and then, if applicable, for an entire set.

This guide is meant as a tool for both the novice and the long-time collector. The novice may think of all postcards as "penny postcards." He may not be aware of the high cost of some rare artist signed cards. The long-time collector may have cards in his collection he purchased many years ago. He may not realize how valuable some of these scarce and desirable postcards have become.

Abeillé, Jack- "Fashion Through the Ages" Signed and dated 1898, no publisher.
Individual postcards-$65 to $85.
Set of six cards- $400 to $450.

Basch, Arpad- "Female Warriors" Signed and dated 1900, no publisher.
Individual postcards-$200 to $300.
Set of six cards-$1200 to $1800.

Bompard, Luigi- "Fashion" Series # 991. Published in Milan, dated 1918.

Individual Postcards-$30 to $40.
Set of six cards-$185 to $200.

Bompard, Luigi-"Leaves of October" Series #515. Published in Milan. Not dated.
Individual Postcards-$40 to $45.
Set of six cards- $250 to $285.

Brunelleschi, Umberto –"Femme" Series #31. Published in France by R&Cie.
Individual Postcards- $300 to $400.
Set of six cards- $2,000 to $2,500.

Brunelleschi, Umberto- "Suffrage" Not numbered. Pub. by Ricordi in Milan.
Individual Postcards-$150 to $200.
Set of six cards- $1,000 to $1,200.

Chiostri, Sofia-"Cherubs and Lady" Series # 245 Pub. by Ballerini & Fratini.
Individual Postcards- $30 to $50.
Set of four cards-$165 to $200.

Chiostri, Sofia- "Bathing Beauty" Series #181. Pub. by Ballerini & Fratini .
Individual Postcards- $40 to $45.
Set of four cards-$175 to $200.

Chiostri, Sofia- "Months of the Year" Series #258. Pub. by Ballerini & Fratini.
Individual Postcards- $40 to $60
Set of twelve cards- $600 to $750.

Corbella, Tito- " Feathers" Series #130. Published in Italy.
Individual Postcards- $20 to $25.
Set of six cards- $125 to $150.

Corbella, Tito- " Turbans" Series #306. Published in Italy.
Individual Postcards- $18 to $25.
Set of six cards- $125 to $135.

Corbella, Tito- " Designs for a Performer" Pub. by Dagami. Series #2109.
Individual Postcards- $22 to $25.
Set of Three cards- $75 to $80.

Danielle, Eva- "Art " Series #2545 Pub. by Raphael Tuck &sons.
Individual Postcards- $285 to $325.
Series, not applicable.

Danielle, Eva- "Modern Art" Series #2525 Pub. by Raphael Tuck & sons.
Individual Postcards- $275 to $300.
Series, not applicable.

Fontan, Léo- "Sheer Stockings" Série #17. Pub. by L-E, Paris
Individual Postcards- $25 to $30.
Set of seven cards- $175 to $225.

Fontan, Léo- " Story of a Pair of Legs" Série #87. Pub. by L-E, Paris.
Individual Postcards- $30 to $35.
Set of seven cards- $200 to $250.

Kirchner, Raphael- "Fashion" Series #235. Pub. by T.S.N.
Individual Postcards- $75 to $100.
Set of six cards- $575 to $650.

Kirchner, Raphael- "Cigarettes of the World" Undivided backs. No #. No Pub.
Individual postcards- $125 to $150.
Set of six cards-$800 to $900.

Koehler, Mela-"Fashion Fabrics" Series #621 Pub. B.K.W.I. Printed in Austria.
Individual postcards- $85 to $150.
Set of six cards- $550 to $950.

Koehler, Mela- "Hats and Fabrics" Series #481.Pub. B.K.W.I Printed in Austria.
Individual postcards- $95 to $225.
Set of six cards- $575 to $650.

Lessieux, Louis- "Precious Stones" Undivided back. No series #. No publisher.
Individual Postcards- $50 to $75.
Set of six cards- $375 to $475.

Mauzan, Luciano- "Fashion" Series #278. Pub. in Milan. Dated 1917.
Individual Postcards- $20 to $25.
Set of six cards- $135 to $165.

Meunier, Henri- "Ladies" Undivided backs. Signed. Pub. Dietrich.
Individual postcards- $85 to $95.
Set of six cards-$550 to $650

Meunier, Henri- "Hairstyles" [Attributed] Undivided backs. Pub. M.M.Vienne.
Individual postcards-$70 to $95.
Set of six cards-$450 to $650.

Montedoro, M.-"Fashion" Pub.in Milan. Dated 1917.
Individual postcards-$125 to $175.
Set of six cards-$800 to $1,100.

Mucha, Alphonse- "Months of the Year" Undivided backs. No publisher.
Individual postcards-$200 to $250.
Set of twelve cards-$2500 to $2800.

Mucha, Alphonse-"Poster of Sarah Bernhardt" Undivided back. No publisher.
Individual postcards-$300 to $350.
Set not applicable.

Mucha, Alphonse- "Designs for a Menu" Undivided backs. No publisher.
Individual postcards-$200 to $250.
Set of four cards-$900 to $1,000

Mucha, Alphonse- "Famous Designs" All undivided backs. No publisher.
"Design for a Fan"- $300 to $350.
"Design for a Soirée Program" - $350 to $400.
"Design for Magazine "Cocorico"-$400 to $450.
"Design for a Calendar"- $250 to $300.

Nanni, Giovanni-"Hats and Fur Scarves" Series #304. Dated 1917. Pub. Milan.
Individual postcards-$20 to $25.
Set of six cards- $135 to $150.

Nanni, Giovanni- "Hats and Good Luck Scarves" Series #284. Pub. in Milan.
Individual postcards- $30 to $35.
Set of six cards- $200 to $225.

Sacchetti, Enrico- "Fashion Designs" Series #25. Pub. by Zeniti. Dated 1917.
Individual postcards-$20 to $25.
Set of six cards- $135 to $150.

Sager, Xavier-"Fashion Designs" Series #8020 Pub. Solomon Bros. London.
Individual postcards-$15 to $20.
Set of six cards-$95 to $120.

Sager, Xavier-"Fashion for Tango" Series #574. Pub. B.G. Paris.
Individual postcards-$20 to $25.
Set of six cards- $125 to $150.

Sager, Xavier-"Fashionable Paris Ladies" Series #545. Pub. B.G.Paris.
Individual postcards-$25 to $30.
Set of six cards-$150 to $180.

Sager, Xavier-"Fashion and Dogs" Small #588, Large #580. Pub. B.G. Par
Individual postcards- $25 to $30.
Set of six cards-$150 to $180.

Sager, Xavier-"The War Years" Series #60. Series #63. Pub. Noyer, Paris.
Individual postcards-$30 to $35.
Set of six cards-$180 to $200.

Sager's Imitators- Mouton. Printed in Paris. No Pub.
Individual postcards-$10 to $15.
Set of six cards-$65 to $95.

Sager's Imitators- Ravok &Robé. Pub. F.F. Paris. No.37

& 40
Individual postcards-$8 to $10.
Set of six cards- $50 to $60.

Schmucker, Samuel L.- "Butterfly Ladies" No series #.
  Pub. Detroit Pub. Co.
Individual postcards- $250 to $300.
Set of six cards-$1,500 to $1,800.

Schmucker, Samuel L.- "Hallowe'en Greetings" Copy-
  righted John Winsch, 1911.
Individual postcards- $225 to $275.
Set of six cards- $1,300 to $1,600.

Schmucker, Samuel L.- "Christmas Greetings" Copy-
  righted John Winsch, 1910.
Individual postcards- $25 to $45.
Set of six cards- $130 to $250.

Solomko, Serge- "Russian Fashion" Pub. T.S.N. (Theodore
  Stroeffer, Nurmberg)
Individual postcards- $10 to $15.
Set of six cards- $65 to $95.

Solomko, Serge- "Fashion of Russian Nobility" Pub. I.
  Lapina, Paris
Individual postcards- $12 to $18.
Set of six cards- $75 to $100.

Steinlen, Alexandre- "Fashion of the Ordinary Lady"
  Undivided backs. No Pub.
Individual postcards- $100 to $150.
Set of six cards-$650 to $950.

Wanke, Alice- " Fashion of Vienna" Series #452. Pub.
  M.M. Vienne.
Individual postcards- $20 to $30.
Set of six cards-$185 to $195.

Unsigned Postcards

Advertising "La Belle Jardinière" Undivided backs. No
  publisher.
Individual postcards- $65 to $85.
Set of six cards- $400 to $500.

Art Deco- (Unsigned) "The Flapper" #353. Pub. J.W.
  Co.
Individual postcards- $9 to $12.
Series not applicable.

Art Deco- " Studies of Two Ladies" Pub.W.R.B, co. Vi-
  enne
Individual postcards- $12 to $22.
Series not applicable.

Art Deco- "Harem Ladies" #211. Pub.by Ballerini &Fra-
  tini in Italy.
Individual postcards-$12 to $15.
Set of six cards- $75 to $90

Art Deco- Fashion "Evening Gowns" No Pub. No num-
  bers.
Individual postcards- $9 to $12.
Set of four cards-$35 to $50

Art Nouveau-"Lady in Corset" Undivided back. Pub.
  Andelfinger & cie.
Individual postcard-$10 to $12.
Series not applicable.

Art Nouveau- "Lady W/Flowers in her Hair" Undivided
  back. Pub. in France.
Individual postcard-$20 to $25.
Series not applicable.

Art Nouveau-"Ladies W/Floral Designs" Undivided backs.
  No pub.
Individual postcards-$20 to $30.
Set of six cards- $150 to $200.

Art Nouveau-"Lady W/Garland of Flowers" Undivided
  back. No Publisher.
Individual postcard- $20 to $25.
Series not applicable.

Pioneer Cards

Pioneer Cards-"Gruss aus Coblenz" Undivided back. No
  publisher.
Individual postcard-$15 to $25.
Series not applicable.

Pioneer Cards-"Greetings from Boston" Undivided back.
  No publisher.
Individual postcard-$25 to $35.
Series not applicable.

Pioneer Cards-"Private Mailing Card" Undivided back.
  No publisher.
Individual postcard- $20 to $25.
Series not applicable.

Pioneer Cards-"Undivided Back" Series # 2535. Pub.
  Raphael Tuck &sons.

Bibliography

Bowers, David and Mary Martin. *The Postcards of Alphonse Mucha.* Perryville, Maryland: Mary Martin, 1980.

Carver, Sally S., *The American Guide to Tuck.* Brookline, Massachusets: Carves Cards, 1976.

Davis, Jack and Dorothy Ryan. *Samuel L. Schmucker: The Discovery Of His Lost Art.* Bozeman, Montana: Olde America Antiques, 2001.

Fanelli, Giovanni and Ezio Godoli. *Art Nouveau Postcards.* New York: Rizzoli Publications, 1987.

Lyons, Forrest D. Jr. *The Artist Signed Postcard.* Gas City, Indiana: L-W Promotions, 1975.

Monahan, Valerie. *An American Postcard Collector's Guide.* United Kingdom: Blanford Press, 1981.

Nicholson, Susan Brown. *The Encyclopedia of Antique Postcards.* Radnor, Pennsylvania: Wallace-Homestead Book Company, 1994.

Ouellette, William. *Fantasy Postcards.* Garden City, New York: Doubleday and Compay, 1975.

Weill, Alain. *Art Nouveau Postcards.* New York, New York: Images Graphics, 1977.

Wood, Jane. *The Collector's Guide to Post Cards.* Gas City Indiana: L-W Promotions, 1984.

Index